THE TEN COMMANDMENTS
-of-
CUSTOMER SERVICE

RICHARD CORRENTE

DENVER, COLORADO

The opinions expressed in this manuscript are solely the opinions of the author and do not represent the opinions or thoughts of the publisher. The author has represented and warranted full ownership and/or legal right to publish all the materials in this book.

The Ten Commandments of Customer Service
All Rights Reserved.
Copyright © 2015 Richard Corrente
v2.0

Cover Photo © 2015 thinkstockphotos.com. All rights reserved - used with permission.

This book may not be reproduced, transmitted, or stored in whole or in part by any means, including graphic, electronic, or mechanical without the express written consent of the publisher except in the case of brief quotations embodied in critical articles and reviews.

Outskirts Press, Inc.
http://www.outskirtspress.com

ISBN: 978-1-4787-4857-1

Outskirts Press and the "OP" logo are trademarks belonging to Outskirts Press, Inc.

PRINTED IN THE UNITED STATES OF AMERICA

Contents

Chapter 1 – Thy ultimate goal is "cash-in-hand" 1
Chapter 2 – Thou shalt "learn-the-need, serve-the-need" 4
Chapter 3 – Thou shalt not Trade dollars for ego. 7
Chapter 4 – Thou shalt Attend to customers – not co-workers. 10
Chapter 5 – Thou shalt not make Thy customer wait. 13
Chapter 6 – Thy customer is always right. NOT! 16
Chapter 6 – (revised) – Thy customer is NOT always right
but thy customer always pays thy bills. 17
Chapter 7 – Thou shalt "Praise-in-Public" And
"Complain-in-Private" 20
Chapter 8 – Thou shalt "Manage problems" Not "Multiply them" 23
Chapter 9 – Thou shalt "Listen-with-amazement;
Speak-with-respect" 25
Chapter 10 – Thou shalt forevermore Have PMS! 27

Customer service is **dead!**

It peaked just after world war two, when people were grateful for your business, respectful of your needs and truly appreciated that contribution you made to putting "food on their table." As a result, sales people were "nice" and businesses prospered.

But as the years went by and automated systems grew in popularity, customer service was gradually replaced with technology and do-it-yourself web sites. E-mails and text messages replaced phone conversations, and the "face-to-face" became all but extinct. (that's why you and I must act NOW!)

Around 2000 (remember the Y-2K fears?) the internet exploded and has continued to grow since then making our economy completely international and the need for human interaction virtually non-existent. The result is the remaining few "customer service representatives" are totally clueless as to what the words mean! Today, as I write this (July 2014), I can honestly declare that customer service is DEAD.

That is a tragedy. But there is a silver lining to the story. Those precious few that understand the overwhelming value and "absolute NEED" for customer service are not just surviving in the worst economy since 1929, they are thriving in it.

You can be part of the problem or part of the solution. The solution is in your hand. If you buy this book, actually read it (very important part of the equation), practice the principles in it and your success, profits, cash-in-hand etc. doesn't improve DRAMATICALLY, I will personally refund double your purchase price! (save your receipt.)

Customer service doesn't have to stay "dead." You can help me bring it back to life. The choice is yours.

CHAPTER 1

Thy ultimate goal is "cash-in-hand"

Every customer service statement you read from this moment forward is designed with this "ultimate goal" in mind. Lose focus of it and failure is guaranteed whether you are a CEO or a waitress. Replace your ultimate goal with your ultimate ego and your business is doomed. Keep it in mind and you and your business CAN'T FAIL! This applies to EVERY business decision you will ever make!

Every decision you make every day; the big ones AND the little ones, need to be guided by this all-important principle. (After all, it is chapter 1) This is why you should always look at yourself from the customers/clients point of view. You are the only person on earth that can NOT give you a profit. Everyone else can! Empathy is a must!

When you answer the phone; when you greet a customer/client for the first time; when you answer his/her questions; when you field his/her complaints; remember how much you love your family and how important it is to bring home as much $$ as you are able to. This sounds so selfish, doesn't it? It sounds like "You're just in it for the money!" Yeah! That's right! You are! You should care about

THE TEN COMMANDMENTS OF CUSTOMER SERVICE

your customers/clients, co-workers, and employers but they should never, ever be more important than your family and loved ones. Your family and loved ones are the very reason you go to work in the first place.

In 1976 I attended a seminar presented by the legendary Tom Hopkins of Tom Hopkins, Champions Unlimited, the number one sales trainer in the United State at that time (and I believe today as well). He asked us to write down how much an hour of our time is worth. So why don't you do that now.

"My time is worth _____ per hour."
Now sign it _____.

Now remember that little voice (that I just put in the back of your head). When it says, "We're wasting time!!" remember that…

"Time is not just like money. Time is money!"

(and how much is an hour of your time worth?)

You will find yourself catering much more to customer service when you remind yourself just how critically important it is (to your family and loved ones) to give the highest possible level of customer service. It's almost like "worshiping" your customer/client.

Your ultimate goal is cash-in-hand. Never, ever, lose sight of your ultimate goal.

Want some help reaching your ultimate goal? Have <u>FUN!</u> Fun is an absolute requirement of reaching your ultimate goal. Tom Hopkins once said "If you're not having fun you're paying too high a price."

If you <u>are</u> having fun it will be more fun for your customers/clients as well. And that connects the circle to increase your income and avoid "having more month at the end of the money" (Tom Hopkins). You may now throw the rest of this book away. (or you can continue because the next chapter has the words that I live by.)

What is your ultimate goal? That's right. Cash-in-hand!

CHAPTER **2**

Thou shalt "learn-the-need, serve-the-need"

These are the words I have lived by throughout my 35 years as a mortgage banker and they apply to EVERY business. The words are so critical that each word deserves to be defined.

"learn" - as in "your customer/client is the teacher and you are the student." Notice it doesn't say "assume", "second-guess", or some other word that suggests that you're so freakin' smart that you don't need to listen. It says <u>learn</u> (damn it) so <u>LEARN</u>!!! Let them finish their sentence. Don't cut them off or complete their thought. Even if you're right it's offensive. God gave you two ears and only one mouth. He did it for a reason! After all; He's God!

"the" — "the'" as in <u>singular</u>. No one has more than one need at a time. They only have <u>one.</u> So stop "multi-tasking" and dividing your focus so much that you aren't paying enough attention to the person who is putting food in your mouth. You'll NEVER get a referral that way. Albert Einstein once said "no person can concentrate on two things as well as one." And he was, well, Einstein! When your customer/client speaks of many needs you have to determine which "one" to serve. Even if you serve several needs, do them one at a time. Being "singular-of-focus" will get you much better results than flattering your ego with "multi-tasking". Customer service means catering to the customer! (not to your inflated ego!) Sorry I'm being a little tough but this one really galls me.

"need"
— not "want", not "desire", not "ego", Learn the NEED! How many times have you heard "want, want, want" from your customer/client. My response usually is "and I want Paris Hilton but she hasn't returned any of my e-mails or text messages!" When the laughter dies down I can usually get my clients to focus on what's important, their "NEEDS." Everyone WANTS a lower price, a faster turnaround, and more for their money. That's why the savy businessperson focuses on their "NEEDS". You should too!

"serve"
— as in the word "servant". Can you be that humble? Can you consider yourself a "servant"? I do. Everyday. I am proud to serve my clients. I recognize that without them I will literally starve to death and I love to eat (lobster is a favorite) so I humble myself EVERY time I speak to customers/clients. It's not easy, I agree, but if you're comfortable with your own self-image and you don't need your ego stroked every 30 seconds then become the servant that your customer/client/master deserves. When you "serve" your people, you'll get to laugh all the way to the bank (and restaurant!).

You'll also be offering a level of customer service your competitors aren't even considering, while they are thinking of new ways to have technology replace customer service. In my neck of the woods we saw the number of mortgage companies decrease from 5,500 to 64! (That's a 99.9% drop in the number of companies and it's even worse because the average size went from about twelve employees to three or four). The remaining few are the ones that survived giving a ton of customer service with technology reserved only for processing the paperwork. "Please and thank you" travel a lot farther that the internet does.

"the" — There it is again. Must be important. Must be a reminder to focus on one thing at a time! Multitaskers multitask because when they mess up they can forgive themselves because they were doing so many things at once so they feel that they don't have to be responsible. Single-taskers (that's a new word I just invented) take responsibility for their actions. Single-taskers actually complete one task rather than have so many that are incomplete that it allows them to forgive themselves when they don't finish a damn thing!

"need" — Sometimes they don't even tell you their real NEED. Sometimes you have to read between the lines. Sometimes you have to be a psychiatrist. People are afraid to open up. They fear telling the complete truth. So they sugarcoat, cover up, pad, polish, and exaggerate. You need to uncover the truth without offending. That takes practice and the technique can only be self-taught. It's different with each one of us. Be patient with yourself. You have to live with you.

Just understand this: If you "learn-the-need-serve-the-need" you will succeed. If you don't you won't.

Now you can throw the rest of this book away. Or not. I'm betting that you keep reading.

CHAPTER **3**

Thou shalt not
Trade dollars for ego.

Humility creates gratuity. Do you have an ego? Are you in love with yourself? Do you cringe when a "bad customer/client calls? (or visits?) Do you send them to voicemail? Do you use derogatory terms to describe them? Would you rather prove yourself right than satisfy the customer/clients needs? Is your need to win the argument MORE important than making the customer/client happy? If you answered "yes" to any of these questions then you are and probably always will be ...a loser! At least until you have an "Aha" moment. You know, that brainstorm that makes you wake up and smell the bankruptcy papers. It's the same defining moment that alcoholics have when they finally decide to go to their first AA meeting. It's the moment when you realize that your customer/client wasn't put on this earth to cater to you, in fact it's the other way around. You are here to cater to them! I read something in the 80's that I posted inside my closet door. It says

EXCELLENCE CAN BE ATTAINED IF YOU CARE MORE THAN OTHERS THINK IS WISE...

◄ THE TEN COMMANDMENTS OF CUSTOMER SERVICE

RISK MORE THAN OTHERS THINK IS SAFE...

DREAM MORE THAN OTHERS THINK IS PRACTICAL...

EXPECT MORE THAN OTHERS THINK IS POSSIBLE.

Your ego is your defense mechanism. It's your shield against the outside world, and you just might believe that world is trying to attack you. Please understand that it's NOT! If you have the courage to "put your ego in your back pocket", you'll find a better world to live in. You'll find the good in everyone. You'll find it easier to give a complement. You'll find it's easier to credit co-workers. You'll find it much easier to edify them to others. And you'll find yourself ignoring their faults. (we all have them). And you'll find a larger paycheck as a result.

I met a man in Massachusetts (we'll call him "Mr. B") who lost it all in the housing crash of 2007 and found a business opportunity that cost $499.00. Problem was he didn't even have the $499.00 so he had a yard sale to raise it. And when he didn't raise enough he had another one. Today he makes about $30,000 a month with his $499.00 investment and when I asked him how he did it he said "I just put my ego in my back pocket and did it." This is a man who realizes that "Money is NOT the root of all evil". He knows that he can take better care of his family if he humbled himself and forged ahead. He refused to "trade dollars for ego". Maybe we should follow his lead.

THOU SHALT NOT TRADE DOLLARS FOR EGO.

Many thanks to "Mr. B".

Back in the early 90's I met a man in Dallas who was a loan originator just like me. His work ethic was almost identical to mine as was his age and work experience. His market was just about a mirror image to Rhode Island where I had been working for the past 15 years. There was, however one glaring difference between us. His W-2 for 1996 was over one million dollars. I saw it. I held it in my hand. I saw his social security number. (I respected him trusting me with that information). My W-2, I promise you, was not. When I listened to him explain why he was so successful, I was amazed. He told me he adopted a phrase "It's all my fault!" and used it every day. That's it! No new technology. No new mailing list. No new Realtor relation techniques. Just "It's all my fault!" Whenever a problem arose he took <u>full</u> ownership of it. He apologized for "causing it" (no matter whose mistake it <u>really</u> was) and worked on solving the issue "he caused." Invariably, the Realtor, the buyer, the seller and everyone else backed off and clearer minds prevailed. Everyone applauded his efforts and his referral base grew expedientially, to a point where he had to hire assistants to handle all his new business . And this makes sense when you think about it. When you take responsibility for <u>whatever</u> goes wrong you invite empathy. Now the customer/client, if they have a heart in their chest, has to defend you. Ninety-nine times out of a hundred they will and the other one time doesn't matter.

So the choice is yours. You can sit on your high (rented) horse or you can refuse to trade dollars for ego and watch your income go up.

Which do you prefer?

CHAPTER 4

Thou shalt
Attend to customers – not co-workers.

Have you ever been in a store, restaurant, office or any customer-service counter and found that the only people receiving "service" were the ones that were supposed to be giving it. Why is it they spend more time talking to each other and taking care of their own agenda rather than helping you with yours?

It's because of a thing called "the comfort zone." All of their co-workers live inside it. You and I (especially me) live outside it. In fact as we approach it you can sometimes read the mind of some of these "insiders." They're saying (sometimes out loud) "Oh no. Here comes another one!" They are "comfortable" interacting with their co-workers. They are loved by them. They know their personality, their likes and dislikes. Their co-workers are supportive and they seldom give rejection, a feeling that no one on this planet wants to feel.

Here's the problem with that. Our paycheck comes from the people who live OUTSIDE of the comfort zone. If we don't make them happy, we fail. And if we don't particularly enjoy failing, when we see a customer/client out of the corner of our eye we should condition ourselves to say "Great, here comes my paycheck!" Not "Oh

THOU SHALT ATTEND TO CUSTOMERS – NOT CO-WORKERS.

hell! I was in the middle of a story with my co-worker and this guy is interrupting!"(By the way, it's one hundred times worse when you continue talking to your freakin' co-worker while the customer/client waits for you to finish!)

When a customer/client opens their mouth we must close ours even if he/she is interrupting us. They have that privilege, WE DON'T! (remember who the "servant" is). Listen intently on what he/she has to say and please, please don't ever try to impress them by second guessing what they are about to say, finish their sentence and then try to answer what you "thought" they were asking. It doesn't work. It doesn't work ever. Not ever! Even if you guess right (fat chance) you will offend them so (as my grandfather used to say) "Shut-uppa-you-mouth" and listen! Remember that two ears and only one mouth thing from chapter two? What the customer/client has to say is not just the most important words of the day, they are the ONLY important words of the day. And whether or not you get paid for today is dependent upon your <u>reaction</u> to his/her words. You can't get paid otherwise. (at least not nearly as much)

There was a waterfront restaurant that had this problem with its wait staff. They would congregate in this five foot by five foot spot next to the kitchen door and enjoy the security and familiarity of each others' company rather than risk rejection from the customers by interacting with them. After complaints mounted the owner took drastic measure. She put a red tape sectioning off that spot and a sign in the kitchen telling the wait staff that if they had the time to "hang around the red tape, they had the time to clean both bathrooms." No one ever stood there again. Customer service skyrocketed. Their customer service was ranked in the top 5% of all restaurants in the area. Sales increased dramatically and the owner was thrilled. The cleanliness of the bathrooms was a different story however, and the health department closed the restaurant down but that's a whole different story.

THE TEN COMMANDMENTS OF CUSTOMER SERVICE

The point is... your co-workers never have and never will pay your bills. Your customers/clients do. Worship them! Kiss their posteriors. They deserve it! And they will reward you with dollars; many, many dollars.

CHAPTER 5

Thou shalt not make Thy customer wait.

There's two parts to this. The first is the initial introduction. Always answer the phone BEFORE the third ring. If the caller has to wait more than three rings to just get someone (and not a machine) to answer the phone they are already annoyed. Then, they hear "You have reached the office of…" or even worse "You have dialed 212-555-0821" Don't they think we know who we just called and what their phone number is??!? I mean, WE JUST CALLED IT! Then, the caller gets "If you want… press extension 101." If you want…press extension 102" (annoying just reading it isn't it?) With phone numbers so inexpensive these days we can eliminate the answering-machine-receptionist, give each employee his/her own phone number (or at least each department), give the caller the impression that we welcome their calls, shoot "customer service quality" through the roof and bury the competition who still use "technology" as poor substitute for human beings.

Next, never leave your paycheck, oops, I meant customer/client on hold for more than seventeen seconds. Please just trust me on this one. Seventeen seconds seems to be the acceptable threshold to stay on hold without being connected or reconnected to a live person. If

◄ THE TEN COMMANDMENTS OF CUSTOMER SERVICE

the caller hasn't reached the party they are calling by then, you just became the receptionist. Get back on the line. Tell the caller how great the person they are calling is (more on that in chapter 7), and keep coming back every seventeen seconds or so. Keeping the caller happy (and yes, entertained) is paramount.

Now, and this is the hard part, disconnect the damn "Voice Mail!". Voice Mail is the single biggest thorn in the side of customer service. Companies that offer superior customer service have statements recorded on their hold button that say "Since we've never installed voice mail, you'll be glad to know that a live person will take your call shortly. Please continue to hold." No one has ever given up when they're on hold waiting for a real live person!

Another plus for a company that refuses to have the dis-service of voice mail is that lazy employees are now forced to actually "speak" to customers/clients! OMG! They actually are forced to give good customer service? What's next? "Please" and "Thank you?" OMG! OMG! Hold on a second. I have to catch my breath. OK, I'm back.

Now for part two. The progress report.

You should call your in-process customer/clients every single day! Even if you have nothing to report. They need to know how important they are and a sixty second phone call lets them know you care.

Customers/clients should never have to wait to get return calls. In 2002 we did a survey and found that of all the people that said they would call, only three percent actually did. Today (2014) we don't need to repeat the survey because no one returns calls. No one. Zero percent! Out of one hundred "Don't call me, I'll call you" promises, absolutely none were kept. I called a charity three times because I wanted to donate money. On three separate days, I left three separate messages asking for a call-back because I wanted to donate

THOU SHALT NOT MAKE THY CUSTOMER WAIT.

$100.00 to that charity. They never called me back! When you offer a hundred dollars for a return call, and you don't get one, something is wrong. Someone should write a book! OK, corny joke, but that's how bad customer service has gotten.

I called 411 on my cell phone the other day and got a recording that said "The Verizon customer you are trying to reach is unavailable at this time" and I'm thinking "I'm paying sixty cents to get them to talk to me and they STILL won't!" Here's the solution. Never let your customer/client call you! That's not a misprint. Never let your customer/client call you. You call them. Be proactive. Call them every day. You can call sixty people in sixty minutes if you don't get longwinded. Leave them a message. Show them you "care more than others think is wise". (see Chapter 3)

Offer them a level of customer service they have never experienced before. Make your personal customer service the "WOW" factor that makes them refer you to everyone and then ask your new BFF to give you the phone number of the referred person because, as we both know, if they give your phone number the referral he/she will NEVER call you. EVER!

OK. Now, finally, you can throw this book away. I have nothing left to say, that is at all intelligent.

CHAPTER 6

Thy customer is always right. NOT!

Thy customer is NOT, I repeat NOT, always right. In fact they are most often wrong and sometimes even very wrong. There, does that make you feel better? It should, because most of you (about 95% by my surveys) feel that way. And you are absolutely RIGHT! But we aren't here to increase your ego are we? We're here to increase your income. We're here to put more dollars in your pocket than ever before, aren't we? So let's make book writing history, you and me. Let's re-title a chapter together. This way it's a team effort. Here goes: (and, by the way, if there is an award for this I promise we will share it!) O.K. Here goes:

CHAPTER **6** – (REVISED)

Thy customer is NOT always right but thy customer <u>always pays thy bills.</u>

For decades I have heard this endless debate of how wrong customers/clients are. They have every right to be as wrong as they want. They are paying for it every time they hand us their hard earned dollars. Remember, they don't have to. They can just as easily hand it over to our competitors. Remember that "humility creates gratuity" from chapter 3? (Wow! You're gonna do great on the final exam!) We don't want to give OUR profits away so always respect that sometimes "life gets in the way" for our customer/clients. We have to respect their opinions, attitudes, criticisms, temperament, mood, anxiety-level, feelings, perceptions, emotions, beliefs, and overall state of mind. You don't know what kind of a day he/she had just before encountering you. You don't know whether or not it was filled with frustration. The ONLY thing you're sure of is that they have our paycheck and we need it to go from their hand to ours. We didn't leave our families this morning to go to work "just for fun." We came to work this morning to collect the money we NEED to pay the bills of our family. Those bills include rent/mortgage, electricity, heat, food, phone, internet, and entertainment. That's how important this customer/client is. He/she literally means "food on the table."

THE TEN COMMANDMENTS OF CUSTOMER SERVICE

For decades I have seen good sales people struggle with the issue of "winning the argument" vs. "winning the sale" and I have a solution.

First, let's determine who is in sales. The answer is ALL OF US. Whether we work for minimum wage at a fast food place or run a fortune 500 company we are <u>ALL</u> in sales. We all sell ourselves either to the public or to our supervisors/bosses etc. every day. And, every day, we have to impress <u>someone</u> to give us money to pay our bills. Whether that is our employer or the general public we sell ourselves to someone, every single day. If we do it well we get a commission. Maybe it's in the form of a complement, or a raise, or an outright commission but we are all in sales of one kind or another.

The problem is we all have an ego too. We all suffer from the sin if "pride." So I have a word for you that I first heard as a "word-to-live-by" in the early 70's. (yes, I'm that old). It was another lesson from Tom Hopkins. (see chapter 1). The word is "empathy". I believe Tom was saying that you don't have to agree with the comment your customer/client is making. Just respect it! Just respect it! (repeated for emphasis). He developed a phrase to bridge the gap on this issue. He says "I appreciate how you feel...." And this is shear brilliance because it respects the words of the customer/client without agreeing with them, a fine line that you must walk on delicately. I have also used the words "I respect how you feel..." but I will stay away from anything that sounds like I'm agreeing with them like "I understand how you feel..." That would certainly cost me money.

The goal here is to never, never offend but if the customer/client is making a statement like "That's too much to pay for something like that" you can offend him/her by saying something confrontational like "No it's not!" or you can empathize with them by saying something respectful like "I appreciate how you feel, however the cost of producing this item has risen. Unfortunately, that's what made the cost go up for us both."

THY CUSTOMER IS NOT ALWAYS RIGHT BUT THY CUSTOMER ALWAYS PAYS THY BILLS.

<u>Empathy.</u> The customer/client deserves empathy. You deserve the customer/clients <u>money.</u> And by the way, money is NOT the root of all evil. The only 2 things money doesn't buy are <u>poverty</u> and <u>disease</u>. Money doesn't <u>guarantee</u> happiness but rich people have happier lives, better homes, better education, better health care, better food, better clothes, better vacations…(can you see a pattern developing here?)

So the customer/client is NOT always right but deserves to ALWAYS be treated with

Empathy!

CHAPTER 7

Thou shalt "Praise-in-Public" And "Complain-in-Private"

I was supposed to go fishing at 2 o'clock today with my brother-in-law Eric. He just called me to say he would be about ten or fifteen minutes late. As he started to tell me why, I told him something I read in a gum wrapper 50+ years ago. I said, " Eric, explain nothing. Your friends don't need it and your enemies won't believe it anyway" But his response is the opening for this chapter. He said "I know but I respect you too much to just let you sit there waiting." This is, in my opinion, the definition of the word "respect." Eric has been like that his whole life. He has two strong personality traits.

1. He always has a kind word (he praises-in-public) and 2. He always seems to be liked by everyone he comes in contact with. (the public praises him). In fact Big Brothers Of America voted him "Big Brother of the Year" in 2012. I wonder if there is a correlation between those two thoughts. I'll bet there is.

Thou shalt: Praise-in-Public:

Do we do this enough? We don't, do we? Why not? Are we afraid people might think we're trying to flatter someone so we can take

THOU SHALT "PRAISE-IN-PUBLIC" AND "COMPLAIN-IN-PRIVATE"

advantage of them? Do we feel that people will assume the negative? In today's economic times the answer, unfortunately, is "Yes." Things are <u>so</u> tough that no one, I mean NO ONE, thinks they deserve praise, or are going to receive it. That's why those true leaders that give it will stand tall in the observers' eyes. Make a sincere complement and people will look at you with more respect than they ever have before. Give someone credit for a task well done and the karma you create will have a positive effect on not only them but you as well. So how do you accomplish this without sounding like you're setting them up? Simple; complement the action, not the person. Something a person <u>did</u>; not something the person <u>is.</u>

"That was a great job!" "That was handled perfectly!" "The customer/client will be really impressed" "Your husband/wife/kids are going to LOVE this!"

After you have mastered this "action-praising" (hey, did we just create another new word?) you can advance to paying direct complements "about" people, but not "to" them. We can agree that it is a lot easier to speak highly about someone if we're not saying it directly to them. Let's create yet another word. We'll call it "people-praising". In public speaking they teach you to "edify, edify, edify, the next speaker." When he/she takes the stage he/she is supposed to "give it back" to you by "edifying, edifying, edifying" you.

When you are speaking to a customer/client about a co-worker always explain how talented he/she is and how fortunate you are to be teamed up with someone as great as he/she is. In this way you are seen as a genuine class act that is grateful for the people around you. When you speak of anyone in your business life speak highly about them or not at all. Openly brag about their accomplishments. Shower them with sincere praise. Tell the customer/client that they have "the best there is" handling their business and your co-worker

THE TEN COMMANDMENTS OF CUSTOMER SERVICE

will be encouraged to do the same. Don't and they won't. Does that make sense?

This "praise-in-public" thing also applies to your competitors but to a lesser degree. I would suggest you say that he/she is "<u>one</u> of the best there is" implying that maybe you are part of that respected group.

Thou Shalt: Complain-in-Private:

I can't stress this enough. Nobody likes a complainer. You don't even like <u>me</u> right now because I'm complaining about.....well....complainers! (I <u>am</u> a complex personality.) But there are occasions when it has to be done. The way to do it successfully is without anyone else but the necessary party or parties hearing or seeing you making the complaint. I don't mean be sneaky about it. I mean be discreet. Respect the privacy of all involved and make your complaint in a well thought out, unemotional and respectful manner. And do it privately, offering a solution, not just a complaint. If anyone overhears you it will be embarrassing to everyone, yourself included, and that might cause more damage than the thing you're complaining about.

Remember the Malthus Theory. (If you don't, here it is). "Never let your solution become more of a problem than your original problem."

and

EDIFY, EDIFY, EDIFY! (Man I love this book!)

CHAPTER 8

Thou shalt "Manage problems" Not "Multiply them"

Back in 1947 the United States had a problem. That is to say our politicians did. They felt we should "monitor the world" to contain the spread of Communism. So they created "The Truman Doctrine" which was "us" giving "us" the right to patrol the world and basically do anything we felt necessary to stem the tide of Communism. (pretty arrogant, don't you think?). Ho Chi Min, in Vietnam took offense to this (what a surprise). The condensed version of what happened next is this:

1954 President Eisenhower stated he felt a danger of "Communism spreading to the USA" and sent Americans to Vietnam to monitor and report Communist activity.

1961 President Kennedy sent the first "honor guard" troops via helicopters to protect the Americans there. They were shot. He sent more troops. They were shot too. He then sent thousands more. The Communists responded by preparing to send nuclear weapons to Cuba. Kennedy sent the entire 9th fleet to surround Cuba in the "Bay of Pigs" invasion. They backed off but relations with Cuba worsened and are still terrible today.

THE TEN COMMANDMENTS OF CUSTOMER SERVICE

1963 Kennedy was assassinated. Many feel the Vietnam war contributed to it.

1964 – 1968 President Johnston escalated the war "beyond all recognition" and the acronym FUBAR (fucked-up-beyond-all-recognition) is created, as well as SNAFU (situation-normal-all-fucked-up).

1968 Finally, Richard Nixon was elected, promising to end the war and in 1969 troops started to be removed. By 1975 they were virtually all gone. Over 20 years of conflict; tens of thousands of lives lost; billions of taxpayer dollars lost, and nothing was accomplished! To this day, no one knows why we were there. Why? There is only one word that I can come up with …EGO.

Ego is what spurs a small problem into an international disaster. So, listen to Mr. "B" in chapter 3 (Hey, you remembered him. Awesome!) and "put your pride in your back pocket".

When a problem arises keep a cool head (even if all around you are losing theirs and blaming you), analyze the issues and decide what needs to be done to REDUCE the drama, not increase it. You may be tempted to spout off and release your frustrations on everyone else but resist!! Stay "singular-of-focus" and solve the problem instead of multiplying it.

You can't keep problems from happening. They're just going to. And problems always seem to follow Murphy's Law. (Simply stated: Nothing is as easy as you thought. Everything will take longer than you expect, and if something *can* go wrong, it *will* go wrong and at the worst possible moment.) All you can do is keep them from becoming the next Vietnam War. Keep your voice calm. Remember your ultimate goal, cash in hand, and thank you in advance for restoring peace in the world that my children and grandchildren live in.

Peace.

CHAPTER 9

Thou shalt "Listen-with-amazement; Speak-with-respect"

I learned what a closing question is from the late J. Douglas Edwards. He defined it as "Any question you ask, the answer to which confirms that fact that he/she has bought!" And then he taught me the most important lesson I have ever learned. (you might want to even write this one down) He said "whenever you ask a closing question ... WHENEVER YOU ASK A CLOSING QUESTION...(and then he shouted at the top of his lungs)

SHUT UP!"

I was in an audience of thousands in Hartford Connecticut. He screamed those words so loud that I never could forget them even if I wanted to. He explained that "if you "shut-up" only 2 things can happen. 1. He/she goes along with you or 2. He/she gives you an objection. Either way, you can cash it in, can't you?" In the 5+ decades I have spent, learning customer service techniques from books, seminars, tapes, videos etc. the most important lesson for

THE TEN COMMANDMENTS OF CUSTOMER SERVICE

me was learning to "shut-up!" Apparently I suffer from "diarrhea of the mouth", a customer service disease that is all too common. I sat in my seat riveted, listening with absolute amazement to one of the greatest public speakers of all time. I thought those words would change my life <u>and they did</u>. When I started to ask a closing question followed by shutting up (my big mouth) things went much better for me AND my customer/client. I vowed then (1973 I think) to always not just listen, but listen with amazement. Everyone has something amazing to say. Whether they are 7 or 70, you gain valuable information when you listen intently. You will be able to cater to their needs better if you listen intently. You will offer a much higher level of customer service when you "listen with amazement". Your customer/client will respect you more and your cash-in-hand will increase as well. (c'mon, you didn't think I'd miss the opportunity to repeat chapter 1 "thy ultimate goal" did you?)

The second half is to "speak-with-respect".

When you speak... and let's face it, you have to say something sometime, speak the way you would like to have the customer/client speak to you. You know; the whole Golden Rule thing. Lower your voice. Be gentle. Be respectful. Be short. Be concise. Don't tell them what you want to tell them. Don't EVER tell them a story that YOU want to hear. Tell them what they "need" to hear. (ooh chapter 2) Imagine yourself bowing to them as you respectfully and sincerely say what you "need" to say. Have empathy (ooh chapter 6!) "Care" (ooh chapter 3) about what they are listening to. Make it worth <u>their</u> while, not yours. Don't forget that God gave you two ears and only one mouth. (ooh you're right! Chapter 2 again!)

You know what? Now you can cancel the final exam. You've already aced it!

Congratulations!

CHAPTER **10**

Thou shalt forevermore Have PMS!

This is it! This is the big finish! This is the last "commandment!"

To be successful; to excel in your customer service; to be all that you can be (sincere apologies the U.S. Army), you must have PMS! That's really all you need to succeed! And you must hold PMS near and dear to your heart and never let it leave your body! Do you have PMS now? If you don't have PMS right now you MUST go out and find it and never, ever let it go. If you have it right now I am happy for you but if you don't, don't worry. We can fix that. Hold it near and dear to your heart for PMS is the greatest gift-from-God and customer service can't possibly exist without it! Those of us who have that wonderfully warm feeling have tremendous success with our customers/clients. Those of us without PMS are doomed to mediocrity. PMS (Positive Mental State) is the lifeblood of customer service and the cure for all that is wrong with business today. If you empower yourself with PMS, every chapter you just read will flow from your voice and your customer service will exceed your wildest expectations. By the way, if you thought PMS meant something besides a Positive Mental State you were horribly, horribly, horribly wrong and your money-back guarantee is hereby null and void. (But still hang on to your receipt. It's still tax deductible) If you don't have PMS here's how you can obtain a lifelong supply.

Be Nice!

Those two words are the hallmark of this book. It's the solution to the problem. It will reincarnate customer service from the "death" I described in the forward. (You did read the forward, didn't you?) Those two words are everything you need to know about customer service. Those two words are actually my religion. No, I'm not trying to change your religious beliefs, just condense them. Think of all the religious rules, guidelines, words of wisdom, proclamations, or commandments of your own religion and they all can fall under the category of "Be Nice!" Bring to mind all that you have ever read about your own religion. If you "Be Nice!" can you violate any part of your particular religious beliefs? If you "Be Nice!" can you go against the Golden Rule, or the 10 Commandments, or the Old Testament, the New Testament or any other religious documents? You can't, can you? So "Be Nice!" and maintain PMS forever!

I knew a lady that made her living "being nice!" (Just for fun we'll give her the fictitious name of "Dawne"). She believed in this principle so much that, in fact, she had a sign behind her desk in her office that said "Because Nice Matters". She went from an entry-level position to Corporate Vice President in less than 2 years and when I asked her how she did this impossible feat she responded "I don't know. I was just nice to everybody." Her exact words. She has 5 kids, a loving husband, and a great career. Not a bad customer service success story from a "Be Nice!" believer. (Maybe we should write a song. We'll call it "I'm a Be Nice! Believer!").

As I come toward the end of this project, and it has been a labor of love, thank you very much, I came across a perfect example of the value of "Be Nice!" I read that on Wednesday August 20th, 2014, a Starbucks customer in St. Petersburg Florida decided to "pay it forward" by paying for the caramel macchiato for the total stranger in the car behind her. That customer followed her good example and paid for the next person and as the employees kept count, a whopping 378 people participated in being "nice." All together 378 people had their lives enriched on that day by this single act of kindness which snowballed into the millions who read the article and it all started with ONE kind person who decided to "Be Nice!" That one person changed the world for the better and you (and I) can too. Albert Einstein once said "Setting an example is not the main means of influencing others, it's the only means." We are all leaders, whether we are a customer at the Starbucks drive-through or the President of the United States. We all must lead-by-example. Our children deserve a better world and this is how we can give them one. All we need to do is "Be Nice!"

God bless you all.

Richard Corrente is available!

For sales training seminars, conventions of any kind, graduations, or any public speaking arrangements.

His fees are variable and extremely affordable; results are money-back guaranteed, and liberal discounts will apply to any worthwhile organizations.

Write to him at:

Richard Corrente 177 Grand View Drive Warwick, Rhode Island 02886

E-mail him at:

rcorrente@123bankers.com

Or better yet, (as the book suggests) just simply call him at:

401-338-9900.

If you have a serious commitment to customer service you're already half way there. Now get hold of Rick to put your team on board.

www.ingramcontent.com/pod-product-compliance
Lightning Source LLC
Chambersburg PA
CBHW020957180526
45163CB00006B/2410